Getting Better

Gill Tanner and Tim Wood

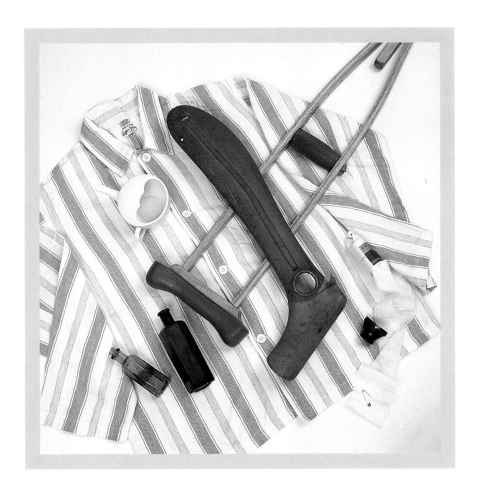

Photographs by Maggie Murray

Illustrations by Pat Tourret

A & C Black · London

Here are some of the people you will meet in this book.

The Hart family in 1990

The Cook family in 1960

Bill Hart

Linda Hart

Kerry

Lee

David Cook

June Cook

Susan

Linda

Andrew

Lee Hart is the same age as you.
His sister Kerry is eight years old.
What is Lee's mum called?

This is Lee's mum Linda when she
was just nine years old in 1960.
She is with her mum and dad,
her brother and her baby sister.

The Smith family in 1930

Richard Smith

Lucy Smith

May

Jack and June

The Barker family in 1900

Charles Barker

Alice Barker

Fred

Harry

Lucy

Amy and Adam

This is Lee's granny June
when she was just a baby in 1930.
Her brother Jack is looking after her.

This is Lee's great grandma Lucy
when she was six years old in 1900.
Can you see what her sister
and her brothers are called?

3

How many differences can you spot
between these two photographs?

One shows a modern child who is ill
and one shows a sick child
one hundred years ago.

This book is about being ill
and getting better.

It will help you find out how
being ill and getting better has
changed in the last hundred years.

There are sixteen mystery objects in this book
and you can find out what they are.
They will tell you a lot about people in the past.

In 1900 the whole Barker family used this
mystery object when they had colds.
It is about the same size as a large mug.
It is made of china with a cork stopper.
The tube in the top is made of glass.
What do you think it is?

Turn the page to find out.

Can you spot the mystery object in this picture?
It is an **inhaler**.

In 1900 people had to pay to see the doctor.
Most families could not afford to call the doctor
each time one of them was ill.
When one of the Barkers had a bad cold,
Alice put a strong-smelling medicine in the inhaler.
Then she filled the inhaler with boiling water.
Fred is breathing in the steam to clear his stuffy nose.

Do you use anything to make you feel better
when you have a bad cold?

You can probably guess
what these two mystery objects are.
They are both made of glass and have cork stoppers.
But do you know why they are coloured
and shaped as they are?
Look carefully. You may spot a big clue.
What do you think went in them?

Turn the page to find out.

Alice Barker is in the chemist's shop.
Can you spot the mystery objects in this picture?
They are **poison bottles**.

In 1900 many people went to the chemist
for help when they felt ill.
Chemists mixed their own medicines.
Some mixtures had a few drops of poison in them.
These were sold in green or blue bottles.
The colours warned people
that they must not drink the liquid.
The bottles were a special shape.
The patterns and letters moulded on the sides
helped people who could not read the labels.

This mystery object is about the same size
as it appears on this page.
It is made of metal wire wrapped in cotton tape.
What do you think it is?

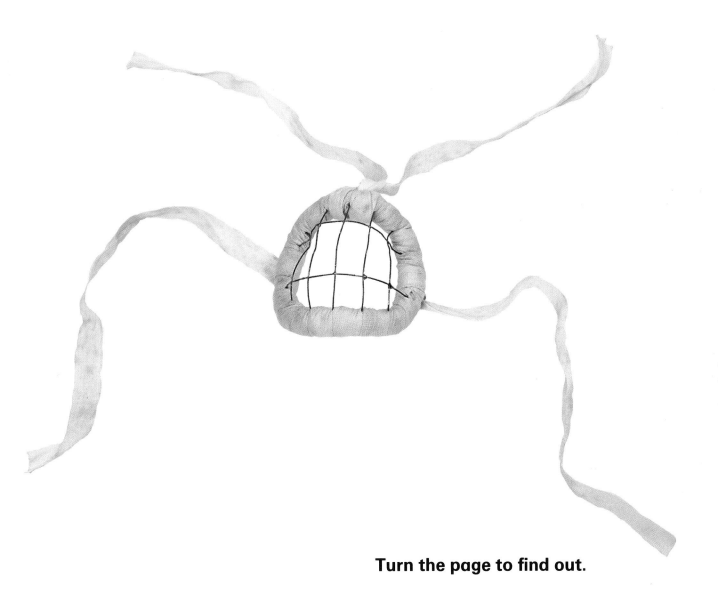

Turn the page to find out.

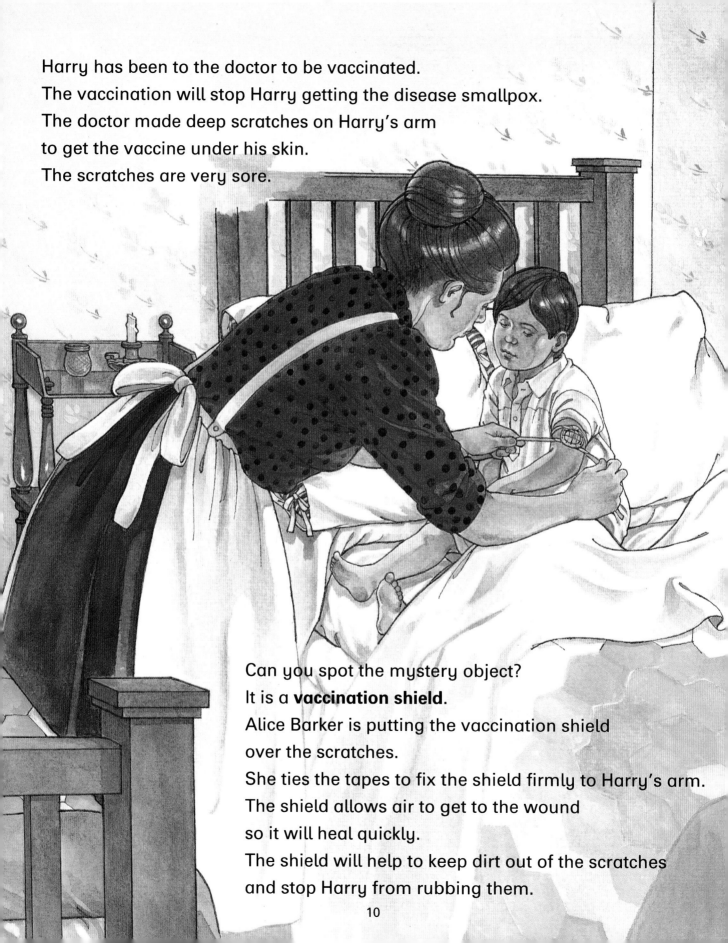

Harry has been to the doctor to be vaccinated.
The vaccination will stop Harry getting the disease smallpox.
The doctor made deep scratches on Harry's arm
to get the vaccine under his skin.
The scratches are very sore.

Can you spot the mystery object?
It is a **vaccination shield**.
Alice Barker is putting the vaccination shield
over the scratches.
She ties the tapes to fix the shield firmly to Harry's arm.
The shield allows air to get to the wound
so it will heal quickly.
The shield will help to keep dirt out of the scratches
and stop Harry from rubbing them.

10

This mystery object is a bit taller than you are.
Most of it is made of metal.
It is a tall stand with a bendy tube at the top.

At the bottom of the stand are a pedal and a wheel.
Can you spot the long, thin cord
which runs from the wheel to the top of the stand?
Can you guess how it works?
Do you know what it is?

Turn the page to find out.

Alice has taken Amy to the dentist.
Can you spot the mystery object?
It is a **dentist's drill**.

The dentist is showing Amy how the drill works.
The nurse is mixing a filling for Amy's tooth.
The dentist rocks his foot on the pedal of the drill
to make the wheel go round.
The wheel turns the cord.
The cord turns a rod inside the bendy tube.
The rod turns the drill at the end of the tube.
Do you have any fillings in your teeth?

The Smiths used this mystery object in 1930.
It is made of china.
It is about the same size as a small teapot.
It worked rather like a teapot too.
Can you guess what it is?

Turn the page to find the answer.

May Smith is ill in bed with measles.
She feels very hot and itchy.
Bright light hurts her eyes.
Can you spot the mystery object?
It is a **feeding cup**.

May is too ill to sit up
and she doesn't feel like eating a proper meal.
Lucy is using the feeding cup to feed May
with soup while May stays lying down.
Lucy holds the spout of the feeding cup to May's mouth.
The curved shape of the top edge of the cup
stops the soup spilling on to May's face.
Do you know anyone who remembers
having the measles?

14

These two mystery objects
were used together.
The white object
is made of a thin cotton material
called gauze.
It is as wide as your hand
and unrolled it would reach across a room.
What do you think the mystery objects were used for?

Turn the page to find out.

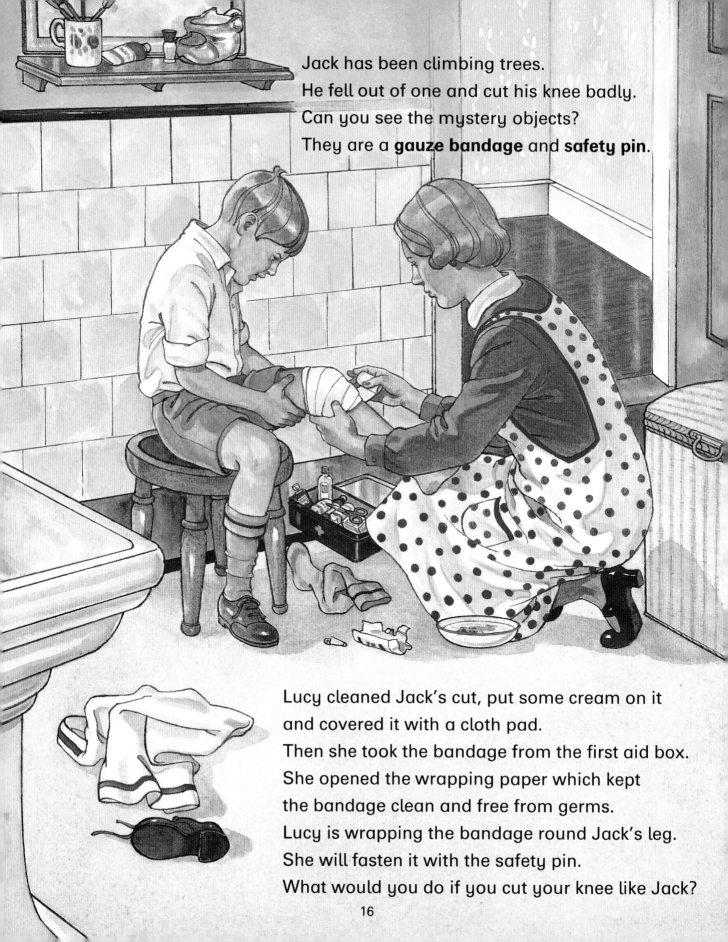

Jack has been climbing trees.
He fell out of one and cut his knee badly.
Can you see the mystery objects?
They are a **gauze bandage** and **safety pin**.

Lucy cleaned Jack's cut, put some cream on it
and covered it with a cloth pad.
Then she took the bandage from the first aid box.
She opened the wrapping paper which kept
the bandage clean and free from germs.
Lucy is wrapping the bandage round Jack's leg.
She will fasten it with the safety pin.
What would you do if you cut your knee like Jack?

16

Andrew Cook used these mystery objects in 1960.
They are made of wood with rubber pads at one end
and in the middle.

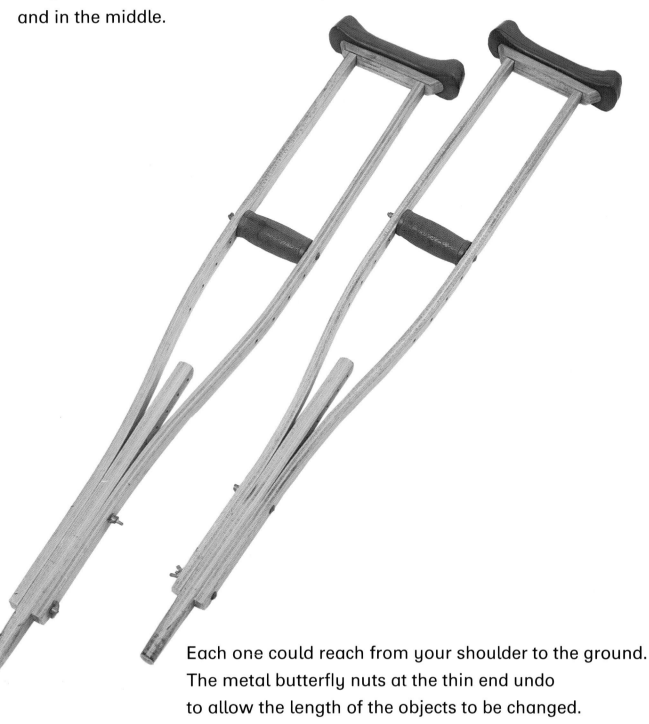

Each one could reach from your shoulder to the ground.
The metal butterfly nuts at the thin end undo
to allow the length of the objects to be changed.
Do you know what they are?

Turn the page to find out.

Andrew has fallen off his bike and broken his leg.
He had his leg put in plaster at the hospital.
Can you spot the mystery objects?

They are a **pair of crutches**.

Andrew holds the handles of the crutches.
He puts the padded tops of the crutches
into his armpits.
He balances with the crutches and hops along.
The crutches mean he doesn't have to use his bad leg.
But Andrew thinks he will not be able
to walk far on the crutches
because they make his armpits sore.

The Cook family used these mystery objects in 1960
when they had colds.
All the objects are used at the same time
and some of them fit together.
One object is rather like a big tin.
It has a lid with a hole in it.
One object looks like a candle.
Can you see the hole for it in the side of the tin?
Where do you think the block fits in the tin?
What do you think the bottle was for?

Turn the page to find out.

Baby Susan has 'flu.
Can you spot the mystery object?
It is a **vaporizer**.
June Cook dropped coal-tar oil from the bottle
on to a small block.
The block soaked up the liquid.
She put the block into the top of the vaporizer
and a night-light into the hole in the middle.

June has lit the night-light which heats the block.
The block gives off a soothing vapour.
June will leave the vaporizer burning all night.
The vapour will help Susan breathe more easily.

Now that you know a bit more about getting better
and how it has changed
over the last one hundred years,
see if you can guess what
these mystery objects are.

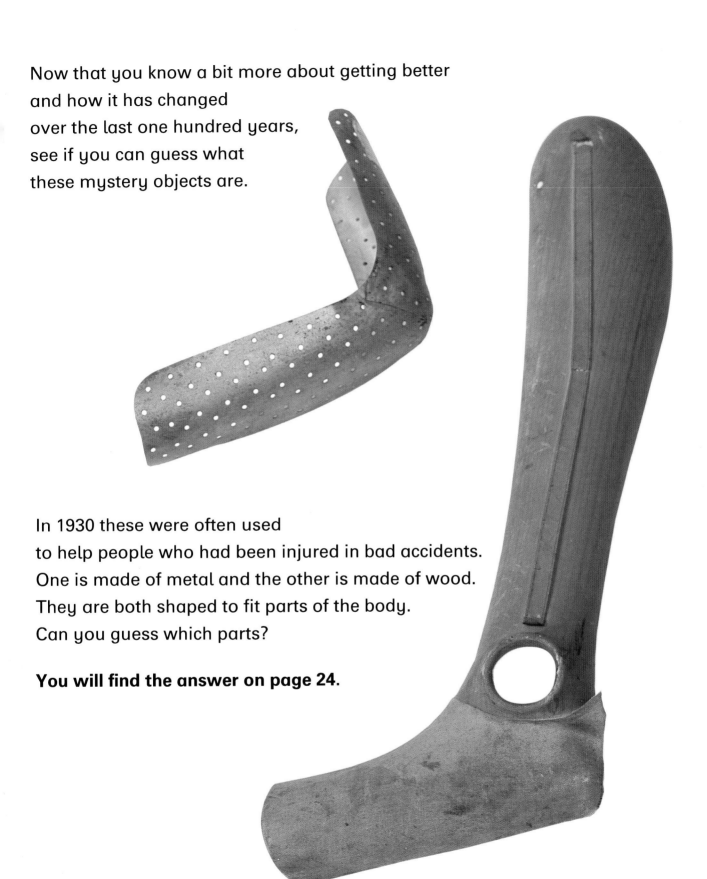

In 1930 these were often used
to help people who had been injured in bad accidents.
One is made of metal and the other is made of wood.
They are both shaped to fit parts of the body.
Can you guess which parts?

You will find the answer on page 24.

Time-Line

These pages show you the objects in this book and the objects we use for getting better nowadays.

1900
The Barker family

inhaler

1930
The Smith family

feeding cup

1960
The Cook family

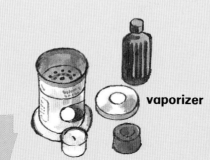
vaporizer

1990
The Hart family

medicines for colds

nasal spray

plastic inhaler

plastic feeding cup

22

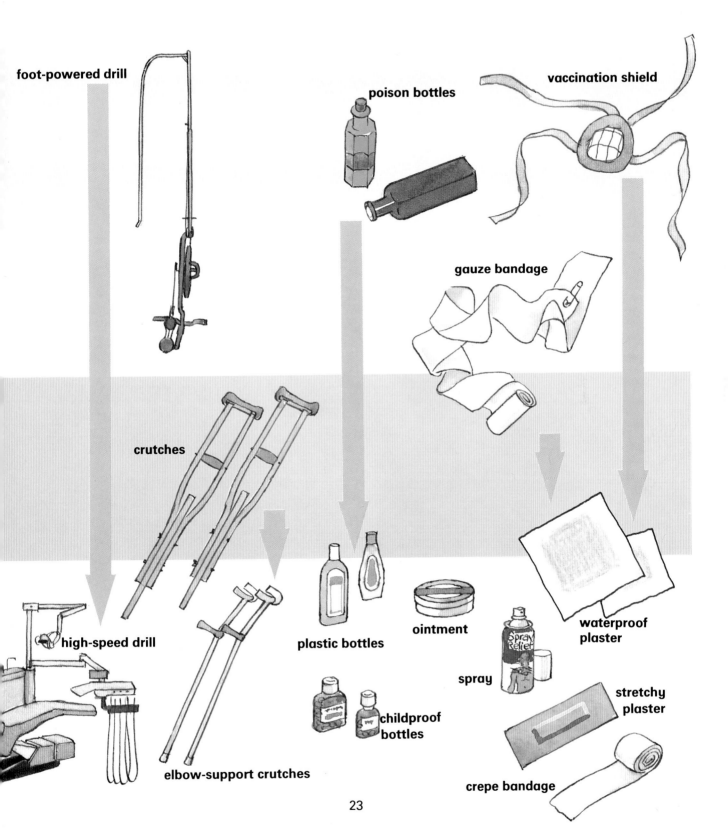

foot-powered drill

poison bottles

vaccination shield

gauze bandage

crutches

high-speed drill

plastic bottles

ointment

waterproof plaster

spray

childproof bottles

stretchy plaster

elbow-support crutches

crepe bandage

23

Index

The **mystery objects** on page 21 are **splints** used in 1930 when June Smith was a baby. Splints keep broken bones still while they mend. The metal splint is for an elbow, the wooden one is for a leg.

For parents and teachers

More about the objects and pictures in this book

Pages 5/6 Friar's Balsam was commonly used in inhalers in 1900.

Pages 7/8 Chemists gave free advice so were preferred by many to doctors, who charged. People might not have been able to read the labels on the bottles because of poor lighting, visual impairment or illiteracy. Some common poison ingredients were opium, camphor oil and strychnine.

Pages 9/10 Inoculation, now called immunisation, had been practised in China and the Arab world for hundreds of years. Vaccination against smallpox was probably first performed by Robert Fooks in 1771. Edward Jenner, who performed his famous vaccination in 1796, was the first to make a systematic practice of this as a method of preventitive treatment. In 1980, smallpox was officially declared to have been eradicated, worldwide.

Pages 11/12 Use of a hand-operated dental drill was first recorded in 1782. The first powered drill, invented in 1863, was driven by clockwork. Electric drills were not invented until 1908. A modern dental drill is driven by air and/or water.

Pages 13/14 Medical treatment still had to be paid for in 1930, so home nursing was a necessity for most families. The National Health Service which gave 'free' medical, dental and hospital treatment to all was introduced in 1948.

Pages 15/16 Gauze probably gets its name from the ancient city of Gaza in Palestine where it was made.

Pages 17/18 Underarm crutches are still used in some cases, but elbow-support crutches are now more common.

Pages 19/20 Coal tar, a by-product of coke production, is a powerful solvent. The vaporizer had to be handled carefully to avoid it catching fire.

Things to do

History Mysteries will provide an excellent starting point for all kinds of history work. There are lots of general ideas which can be drawn out of the pictures, particularly in relation to the way medical treatment, clothes, family size and lifestyles have changed in the last 100 years. Below are some starting points and ideas for follow up activities.

1 Work on families and family trees can be developed from the family on pages 2/3, bearing in mind that many children do not come from two-parent, nuclear families.

2 Find out more about illness and getting better in the past from a variety of sources, including talks by or interviews with older people in the community, chemists, doctors, as well as books and museums. Illness and getting better weren't the same for everyone. Why not?

3 There is one object which is in one picture of the 1900s, one picture of the 1930s, and one picture of the 1960s. Can you find it?

4 Arrange a field trip to a museum, such as the Jenner Museum in Gloucestershire or the Wellcome Museum in London.

5 Look at the difference between the photographs and the illustrations in this book. What different kinds of things can they tell you?

6 Make your own collection of medical objects or pictures. You can build up an archive or school museum over several years by encouraging children to bring in old objects, collecting unwanted items from parents, collecting from junk shops and jumble sales. Likely objects might be old first aid boxes, and empty bottles and jars. Sharp items or old medicines should not be handled by children and must be disposed of safely by an adult. You may also be able to borrow handling collections from your local museum or library service.

7 Encouraging the children to look at the objects is a useful start, but they will get more out of this if you organise some practical activities which help to develop their powers of observation. These might include drawing the objects, describing an object to another child who must then pick out the object from the collection, or writing descriptions of the objects for labels.

8 Encourage the children to answer questions. What do the objects look and feel like? What are they made of? What makes them work? How old are they? How could you find out more about them? Do they do the job they are supposed to do?

9 What do the objects tell us about the people who used them? Children might do some writing, drawing or role play imagining themselves as the users of different objects.

10 Children might find a mystery object in their own house or school for the others to draw, write about and identify. Children can compare the objects in the book with objects in their own home or school.

11 If you have an exhibition, try pairing old objects with their nearest modern counterparts. Talk about each pair. Some useful questions might be: How can you tell which is older? Which objects have changed most over time? Why? What do you think of the older objects? What would people have thought of them when they were new?

12 Make a time-line using your objects. You might find the time-line at the back of this book useful. You could include pictures in your time-line and other markers to help the children gain a sense of chronology. Use your time-line to bring out the elements of *change* (eg. the development of medical knowledge leading to more effective treatments, the introduction of a national health service, the increasing emphasis on prevention rather than cure, particularly the ability to immunise against common infections such as measles, improved hygiene, living conditions and public health, hi-tech medicine, the conquest of pain) and *continuity* (eg. the continuing existence of illnesses, home treatment etc).

History Mysteries

First published 1994
A & C Black (Publishers) Limited
35 Bedford Row, London WC1R 4JH

ISBN 0-7136-3803-6

© 1994 A & C Black (Publishers) Limited

A CIP catalogue record for this book is available
from the British Library.

Acknowledgements

The authors and publishers would like to thank Suella Postles and the staff of Brewhouse
Yard Museum, Nottingham; Mrs Tanner's Tangible History; Mike Greenwood, Dental
Adviser Nottingham;
Cara Bozarth; Veena Jackson; Dr J. Conway; Dr G. Urwin.

Photographs by Maggie Murray except for: p4 (top) Roshini Kempadoo; p4 (bottom)
Format.

Filmset by Rowland Phototypesetting Limited, Bury St Edmunds, Suffolk
Printed and bound in Italy by L.E.G.O.